W9-CFG-881

INSECTS & SPIDERS

PESTS &
PARASITES

Per Christiansen

Gareth Stevens
Publishing

Please visit our web site at **www.garethstevens.com**
For a free color catalog describing Gareth Stevens Publishing's
list of high-quality books, call 1-800-542-2595 (USA)
or 1-800-387-3178 (Canada).
Gareth Stevens Publishing's fax: 1-877-542-2596

Library of Congress Cataloging-in-Publication Data
available upon request from publisher.

ISBN-10: 0-8368-9218-6 (lib. bdg.)
ISBN-13: 978-0-8368-9218-5 (lib. bdg.)

This North American edition first published in 2009 by
Gareth Stevens Publishing
A Weekly Reader® Company
1 Reader's Digest Road
Pleasantville, NY 10570-7000 USA

Copyright © 2009 by Amber Books, Ltd.
Produced by Amber Books Ltd., Bradley's Close
74–77 White Lion Street
London N1 9PF, U.K.

Illustrations © International Masters Publishers AB

Project Editor: James Bennett
Design: Tony Cohen

Gareth Stevens Senior Managing Editor: Lisa M. Herrington
Gareth Stevens Editor: Joann Jovinelly
Gareth Stevens Creative Director: Lisa Donovan
Gareth Stevens Designer: Paul Bodley

Printed in the United States of America

1 2 3 4 5 6 7 8 9 10 09 08

Contents

Continents of the World

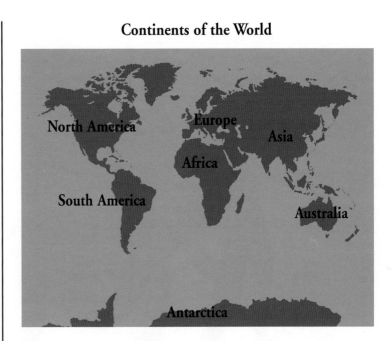

The world is divided into seven continents — North America, South America, Europe, Africa, Asia, Australia, and Antarctica. In this book, the area where each animal lives is shown in red, while all land is shown in green.

Words that appear in the glossary are printed in **boldface** type the first time they occur in the text.

Aphid

The aphid has a large, round **abdomen**, or lower body. The abdomen is divided into sections.

Like other insects, the aphid has six legs, three on each side of its body.

The aphid's legs end in tiny claws that help it grip surfaces. It also uses its claws to explore and search for food.

The aphid has long **antennae** that stick out of its head. It uses them to sense which plants are good to eat.

The aphid does not have biting **mouthparts**. It uses a long, hollow tube to suck juices from leaves.

Aphids have an unusual life cycle.
(1) In summer, a female aphid gives
birth to smaller copies of herself, called
clones. (2) A winged female clone flies from one
plant to another. (3) In fall, she gives birth to
male and female clones. A male aphid then
mates with a female. (4) The female lays eggs
and attaches them to the plant stem.
(5) In spring, the eggs hatch into female **nymphs**.
(6) Each female adult then produces more female
clones, including a winged female.
(7) The winged female flies to
another plant to begin the
cycle again.

Size

x10

Where in the World

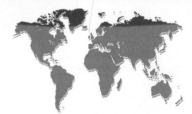

Aphids live all over the world. They are found in **temperate** and **tropical** areas.

5

Aquatic Leech

A leech has a sucker at both ends of its body. The smaller sucker is actually the leech's head! This sucker cannot be used for sucking blood.

Many **muscular** rings line the leech's body. Its skin is tough and leathery.

A leech has a large sucker at the end of its body. This sucker has a mouth with many small, sharp jaws. The jaws allow the leech to saw through the skin of large animals, such as horses, to get to their blood.

A leech can really stretch. When it is resting, it looks almost round. Then it stretches its body and begins crawling by using its suckers.

Most leeches are small and can stretch only up to 2 inches (5 centimeters). Some larger types can reach a length of 6 inches (15 cm). Long ago, doctors used leeches to drain "bad" blood from patients because they thought doing so could cure diseases.

1 Leeches feed on the blood of fish or large, warm-blooded animals. As this horse drinks from a lake, a leech grabs hold of its skin.

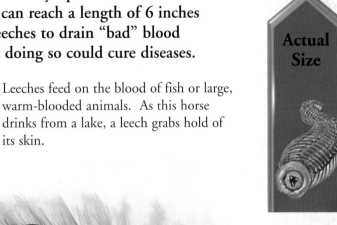

2 The leech uses its jaws to saw a hole in the horse's skin. When the blood flows, the leech spits up a liquid to stop the blood from **clotting**. Then it drinks its fill.

Actual Size

Where in the World

Leeches live in lakes, streams, and wetlands across much of the world.

7

Bedbug

The bedbug uses its long antennae for smelling and feeling the world around it. The body heat of warm-blooded animals attracts bedbugs.

The bedbug has a large, flat body. When it **gorges** on blood, its body becomes plump and round.

The bedbug has a long, pointed tube for a mouth. Most bugs use tube mouths for sucking plant juices. Instead, bedbugs suck the blood of warm-blooded animals.

The bedbug has three pairs of long, skinny legs. It moves slowly and creeps up on its victims!

Bedbugs can live for more than a year. They usually suck blood once every week or two during their lives. Adult bedbugs are about the size of a sesame seed. Small bedbugs are almost clear and can be difficult to see.

 1 The bedbug is attracted to the warmth of a person's body and to the **carbon dioxide** in his or her breath. The bedbug is active in the early morning, when it slowly climbs onto its prey.

Size

x5

Where in the World

Bedbugs live all over the world, mainly in temperate climates.

 2
The bedbug uses its long tube-like mouth to punch though the person's skin and suck blood.

3
The bedbug's stomach can hold up to five times its weight in blood. As the bedbug feeds, its body swells and it turns from brown to purple.

Kissing Bug

Adult kissing bugs have wings. They live inside the nests of birds and small animals such as armadillos and opossums. During the night, kissing bugs often fly to different nests.

The kissing bug has a long, flat body. It got its name because it likes to bite around a person's eyes and mouth. The bites are painless and often occur while people sleep. Bites from kissing bugs can spread disease.

The kissing bug's mouth is a long, sharp tube. The bug uses the tube to pierce its victims' skin and suck their blood. Once the kissing bug's body fills with blood, it becomes fat.

The kissing bug has three pairs of long, skinny legs. It hides during the day and becomes active at night.

Adult kissing bugs can reach almost 1 inch (2.5 cm) in length, including their long tubes. Young nymphs are much smaller.

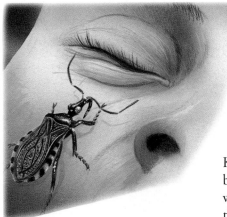

1 Some kissing bugs live inside houses. They seek their sleeping victims at night.

2 Kissing bugs bite skin only where it is thinnest, often near the eyes or mouth.

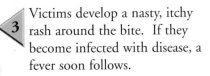

3 Victims develop a nasty, itchy rash around the bite. If they become infected with disease, a fever soon follows.

Actual Size

Where in the World

The kissing bug lives in the southern United States and in Central and South America.

Chigger Mite

The chigger mite is a distant relative of spiders and scorpions. Like those **arachnids**, adult chigger mites have eight legs. Adult chigger mites do not bite.

The chigger mite has a wide, triangular abdomen. Its skin is tough and leathery. Chigger mites are attracted to peoples' body heat. They are also drawn to the carbon dioxide in their breath.

The chigger mites that bite humans are larvae. Since they have recently hatched from eggs, they have only grown six of their eight legs.

Chigger mites come in many colors. Most are orange or red. Tough, spiny hairs cover their bodies and legs.

Chigger mites are barely visible to the naked eye. They look like tiny red dots crawling on a person's skin.

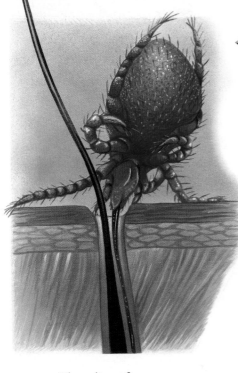

1 ▷ The chigger mite burrows into its victim's skin around the base of a hair shaft. It sucks the victim's blood. The chigger mite injects **saliva** into the wound to prevent clotting.

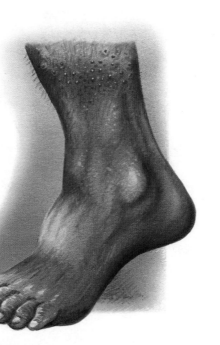

2 ▷ The saliva often causes a victim's skin to feel sore and itchy. In some instances, redness and swelling may occur.

Colorado Potato Beetle

The Colorado potato beetle exposes its soft abdomen when flying. Its abdomen is divided into segments.

The Colorado potato beetle has a pair of soft, clear wings for flying.

Hard **wing cases** protect the potato beetle's body. They lift away from the body only when the beetle flies. Wing cases are actually **modified** wings, and only beetles have them.

Yellow and black stripes cover the potato beetle's wing cases and body. Its bright coloring warns predators that the beetle's body contains bad-tasting chemicals.

The Colorado potato beetle is a half inch (1.2 cm), or about the size of a ladybug. The red-colored larvae are much smaller.

1 Adult beetles lay their eggs on the leaves of potato plants. The eggs hatch into tiny larvae.

2 The larvae eat the plant's leaves. In some years, beetles destroy large fields of potatoes.

3 When the larvae are grown, they drop to the ground and **pupate**.

Adult beetles hatch from the **pupae** the following year. 4

Actual Size

Where in the World

The Colorado potato beetle lives in North America, Central America, and Europe. It also lives in parts of Asia and Africa.

Dust Mite

The dust mite has a fat, rounded body and a tough skin.

Female dust mites look extremely fat because they have up to 100 eggs inside their bodies. After the female dust mite lays her eggs, they will hatch into tiny larvae in about a month.

Like spiders and scorpions, the dust mite is an arachnid. It has biting mouthparts and eight short, thick legs.

Most of the dust mite's body is made up of chambers to store food. Its **digestive system** is simple, so it must take in large amounts of food to get energy.

Dust mites are so tiny that they are almost invisible to the naked eye. Adult dust mites are about half the size of the period at the end of this sentence.

Size

x125

2 Dust mites have chambers, not stomachs. Special chemicals in their digestive system break down their food.

1 Dust mites eat small flakes of skin, which people shed every day. The mite chews the skin flakes with its mouthparts.

3 Dust mites eat their own waste several times to digest it. Their **dung** comes out in tiny bits and makes up much of the dust in houses.

Where in the World

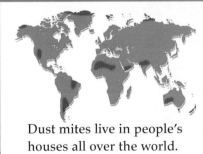

Dust mites live in people's houses all over the world.

Hard Tick

This female tick's huge abdomen contains eggs. She needs fresh blood to help her eggs grow until they are ready to be laid.

This female hard tick is full of blood, so her body is round and fat. A hard tick normally has a small, flat abdomen. All hard ticks have a thick outer shell.

Hard ticks are arachnids. They have eight legs that are short and fat.

The tick has a small head with a long, hollow tube for a mouth. Curved spines line the tube. These spines stick into the skin of a tick's victim, making the tick difficult to remove.

Adult male ticks are a few millimeters long, and females may be slightly larger after they have gorged themselves on blood.

1 Ticks climb to the tip of blades of grass or small twigs. Here, they sit and wait. When an animal or a person passes by, ticks jump on.

Size

x4

Did You Know?

Hard ticks are attracted to the carbon dioxide in human breath. Small ticks only suck the blood of mice, but larger adult ticks attack deer, foxes, dogs, and humans.

2 The tick buries its entire head in the victim's skin. It then releases saliva, so the blood cannot clot. Then the tick begins to suck blood. After one to two days, it is full and drops off. The saliva may contain dangerous **bacteria** that can cause illnesses such as Lyme disease.

Where in the World

Ticks live across most of the world except near the North and South poles.

Human Louse

The louse has long, hollow, tube-like mouthparts. It uses these tubes to pierce human skin and suck blood.

The human louse is an insect that has six legs.

The louse's legs end in pointed tips that help it cling to skin and hair. Lice pass from victim to victim when they touch.

The louse stores the blood in its long abdomen. In young lice, this blood makes the abdomen red, giving them the nickname "red-backs."

Human lice are tiny insects. The human head louse is smaller and more slender than the human body louse. Both reach lengths of up to 0.12 inches (3 mm).

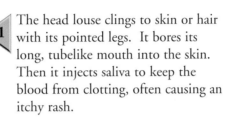

1 The head louse clings to skin or hair with its pointed legs. It bores its long, tubelike mouth into the skin. Then it injects saliva to keep the blood from clotting, often causing an itchy rash.

2 Body lice are well adapted for clinging to human hair and are difficult to remove. Their six legs point inward and end in short, sharp claws. The louse can grab onto a hair almost as a human hand does.

Size

x7

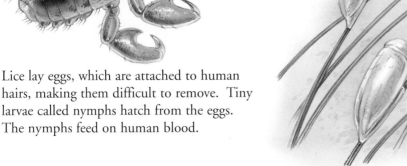

3 Lice lay eggs, which are attached to human hairs, making them difficult to remove. Tiny larvae called nymphs hatch from the eggs. The nymphs feed on human blood.

Where in the World

Human lice live everywhere in the world where people do.

Chigoe Flea

The chigoe flea has a long, thin body.

Fleas suck the blood of warm-blooded animals. The chigoe flea uses its jagged jaws to bite through an animal's skin. Then it feeds on the animal's blood.

All fleas have long back legs. They use them to jump hundreds of times their own length.

Fleas have stiff hairs around the sides of their heads. Scientists can identify different types of fleas by their hair.

Chigoe fleas are smaller than other types of fleas. They are about 0.03 inches (1 mm). Chigoe fleas are also called sand fleas. They live in tropical, sandy areas, such as beaches.

Chigoe fleas attack animals such as mice, dogs, cows, horses, and humans.
(1) Here, a female flea burrows into the skin underneath a human toenail.
(2) The only sign of its attack is a red patch of skin.
(3) The flea sucks the person's blood. Within days, the flea swells to the size of a pea. Its eggs feed on the person's blood. Once the eggs are laid, the tick dies.

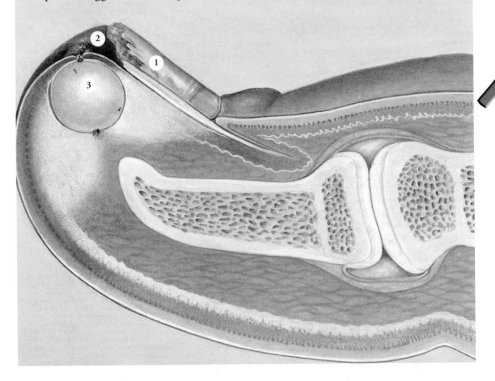

Size

x10

Where in the World

Chigoe fleas live in tropical areas. They are common in South America and Africa.

Scabies Mite

Long, stiff hairs cover the mite's short, fat body. It also has shorter spines on its body. These spines help the mite tunnel through the skin.

Scabies mites are arachnids. They are related to spiders. Their eight short legs are good at tunneling under skin.

The scabies mite's wide head has biting mouthparts. The mite uses its mouthparts to tunnel through the skin and feed on it.

With such thick legs, scabies mites cannot run or jump. They infect a new victim by direct skin-to-skin contact.

Scabies mites are tiny. They are barely visible to the naked eye.

1 Scabies mites burrow into a person's flesh. They tunnel through the skin, feeding on it for several days.

2 Female scabies mites lay eggs inside the skin tunnels, increasing the number of mites. They spread through the skin and multiply rapidly. Scabies mites attack fingers, wrists, armpits, waists, and thighs.

Size

x35

Did You Know?

An attack of scabies is incredibly irritating for humans, but it can be easily treated. In animals, scabies mites can cause **mange**, a terrible disease. For wild animals such as foxes, mange can cause hair loss, skin infections, and even death.

Where in the World

Scabies mites live across much of the world.

Termite

Worker termites often have large heads for powerful biting. Some workers, such as this one, are larger and have enormous heads. They are called soldiers. Their job is to defend the colony against enemies. The smaller workers gather food.

The termite's short, six-legged body is divided into segments. Special bacteria in the termite's intestines help it digest wood.

Termites live in groups called colonies that have a distinct social order. Termites can be nymphs, workers, soldiers, kings, or queens. Only king and queen termites can mate. They are the only termites with wings.

All worker termites have strong jaws for gnawing wood. Soldier termites have huge jaws, which they use only for fighting.

Termites vary in size. Some **species** are only a few millimeters long. The largest African termites can grow to more than 1 inch (2.5 cm). Their queen can grow to be 4 inches (10 cm) long!

1 Termites live in nests underground and are rarely seen. This man is delivering a package to a house. He does not realize that termites also live there!

2 Termites have tunneled through the boards on the porch, making them hollow and fragile. This unlucky man finds out the hard way!

Where in the World

Termites live all over the world but are most common in tropical areas.

African Armored Cricket

The African armored cricket got its name because of its tough, armored skin and sharp spines. Predators, find the crickets difficult to eat.

The African armored cricket has powerful back legs for jumping. It can get rid of enemies by kicking them.

Crickets have large eyes and good eyesight.

The cricket's long, skinny legs end in two sharp claws. These claws enable it to get a strong foothold on most surfaces.

The cricket's large, powerful jaws can chew tough plants.

An adult female armored cricket can grow to more than 2 inches (5 cm). The long, egg-laying tube at the end of its body adds an additional inch (2.5 cm) to its length.

Size

The African armored cricket eats plants. It is sometimes considered a pest to crops. These crickets also like meat—including flesh from their own kind. This cricket has stopped to eat a cricket that has been run down by a vehicle.

Where in the World

The armored cricket and its close relatives live in Africa.

Glossary

abdomen — the lower section of an insect's body

allergies — the reactions of a person's body against certain substances such as dust

antennae — a pair of long feelers on an insect's head

arachnids — group of eight-legged animals that includes spiders, scorpions, and mites

asthma — a condition that causes wheezing and coughing and that makes breathing difficult

bacteria — tiny living things that can cause diseases

carbon dioxide — a colorless gas that animals and people exhale

clones — copies of something that closely resembles the original

clotting — to stop a flow of liquid such as blood and form a mass or lump

cocoon — sacs, pouches, or cases that help protect an insect's larvae before they change into adults

digestive system — the group of organs, including the stomach and intestines, that breaks down food and changes it into energy

dung — the waste material from animals

gorges — drinks in large amounts

larvae — young, developing insects

mange — a disease caused by parasitic mites that can result in hair loss and skin infections

mates — joins together to produce babies

modified — changed

mouthparts — the parts of an insect used for feeding

mucus — a thick, jelly-like liquid made by an animal to protect its body

muscular — having a lot of muscle, the material that gives the body strength

nymphs — insects that have not completely developed

parasites — animals that feed off other live plants and animals

predators — animals that hunt other animals for food

pupae — insects in the stage between larvae and adults

pupate — to change from larvae to cocooned pupae

saliva — a liquid made in the mouth, containing water, protein, and salts

species — a group of living things of the same family

temperate — marked by temperatures that are neither very hot nor very cold

tissue — a layer or mass of one kind of cell

tropical — referring to the hottest parts of the world, with lush plant life and lots of rain

wing cases — hard coverings that protect an insect's delicate flying wings

For More Information

Books

The Bug Scientists. Scientists in the Field (series). Donna M. Jackson (Houghton Mifflin, 2004)

Cockroaches. Gross Bugs (series). Jonathan Kravetz (Rosen/PowerKids Press, 2006)

Head Lice Up Close. Minibeasts Up Close (series). Robin Birch (Raintree, 2004)

The Most Extreme Bugs. Animal Planet Extreme Animals (series). Catherine Nichols, editor (Jossey-Bass, 2007)

What Lives Under the Carpet? What Lives In…? (series). John Woodward (Gareth Stevens, 2002)

What's Living on Your Body? Hidden Life (series). Andrew Solway (Heinemann Library, 2004)

Web Sites

Live Science — All About Insects
www.livescience.com/insects

Pest Patrol — A Backyard Activity Book for Kids
www.epa.gov/pesticides/kids/pestpatrol/index.htm

Pest World for Kids
www.pestworldforkids.org/home.asp

Super Sleuth Resources — For Kids
www.ipminstitute.org/Super_Sleuth/Resources/ homework_resources_kids.htm

Very Cool Bugs — Bug Bios
www.bugbios.com/entophiles/index.html

Index